PRAISE FOR

RAMSHACKLE ODE

"If you want to know what the good, serious work—by
which I mean digging and plowing and axing and building
and sewing and holding—of joy—which includes, yes,
no kidding, sorrow, loss, heartbreak, the whole abundant
mess—might make of the world, of a family, of a
life—*goddamn, goddamn*—I think this book might give you
an idea. It's kind of the hardest work, joy. Which makes
Ramshackle Ode one of the hardest-working books I've
read in a long time."

— ROSS GAY

"*Ramshackle Ode* is a brilliant, heartbreaking, sometimes
funny, always surprising celebration of love and attachment,
of all the ways our connection to others—friends, lovers,
children—makes us hostages to fortune. The force of
imagination and the urgent desire to praise, care for, and
cultivate is always at every point tested by the equal force of
depredation and defilement. This is a terrific and memorable
first book. Leonard's voice is powerfully distinct and fresh,
and it's one I'm sure we'll be hearing with gratitude for
years to come."

— ALAN SHAPIRO

"*Ramshackle.* Synonyms: *neglected, gone to rack and ruin, beat-up*—and aren't we? Isn't our house in tumbledown? Some days it seems it's all getting to be too much now, that you're beat up just by living. *Ramshackle Ode* is more than a great book of poems; it's a tent revival, a people's sweaty redemption. Keith Leonard has come right in the nick of time to remind us that inside each our hearts thumps an ecstatic hot night of healing, and raise that tambourine! — hallelujah be, there's still a song, goddamnit there's still a chance to sing."

— REBECCA GAYLE HOWELL

"Poetry is the ages-old means to see beyond, to glimpse what's out there and to praise even what we don't yet know. These poems do not linger on grief; instead, they reveal a heart that has been opened to love and a mind flung out to wonder. That is the solemn human journey. No rest for the wicked, is the common expression. No rest for the joyful and compassionate either. That is the discovery these poems field, like pop flies and grounders in a backyard baseball game played so long ago in youth it has the resonance of myth. These poems have earned their wisdom, and this book is a gift I happily hold in my hands."

— MAURICE MANNING

RAMSHACKLE ODE

RAMSHACKLE

ODE

KEITH

LEONARD

MARINER BOOKS

HOUGHTON MIFFLIN HARCOURT

BOSTON

NEW YORK

2016

For information about permission to reproduce selections from this book,
write to trade.permissions@hmco.com or to
Permissions, Houghton Mifflin Harcourt Publishing Company,
3 Park Avenue, 19th Floor, New York, New York 10016.

WWW.HMHCO.COM

Library of Congress Cataloging-in-Publication Data is available.
ISBN 978-0-544-64967-5

Book design by Mark R. Robinson

PRINTED IN THE UNITED STATES OF AMERICA
DOC 10 9 8 7 6 5 4 3 2 1

Excerpt from "Night" from *The Blue Estuaries* by Louise Bogan.
Copyright © 1968 by Louise Bogan. Copyright renewed 1996 by Ruth
Limmer. Reprinted by permission of Farrar, Straus and Giroux, LLC.

for Jen and Noah

—O remember
In your narrowing dark hours
That more things move
Than blood in the heart.

—LOUISE BOGAN,
from "Night"

CONTENTS

— — — — — — — — — — —
— — — — — — — — — — —

RAMSHACKLE ODE

KEEL

That half-moon smooth beam,
I think someone made it because
they had a spine and wanted
to make a stronger one,
and they sent the little skiff
out to sea for years,
and it went on boot-thudded
and shoal-scraped,
and it went on boot-thudded
and shoal-scraped, and it held
all the while like it holds
in the boatyard, though
it is belly-up on blocks
to keep out the rain, now,
and it does rain here,
and did again this morning
when I was walking your dog,
Love, thinking how I, too,
have been boot-thudded

by love, I was my own
storm once, so young
and eager to raise the sail
of my wanting, and I just wanted
to tell you I love this old boat,
this settled-in thing.

THE

DOUBLING

Though the rain tastes like nickel
it is not blood, but like blood
makes the child, rain plumps
the melons beneath thick leaves
this summer, and each summer,
and it's a genius I rarely think of,
this world swelling, the hay field
rising, and I was not ready
for my love to be suddenly
amplified by the ultrasound,
but it was, the little heart drummed
over the speakers, and the room
swelled, and it hurt the good hurt,
and though the June bugs
beat against the night, the sound
is not a heart, but like the heart
it is dumb in its brazen pulse
and smack-the-screen joy,
and like the heart there are billions

here, each alive and mostly well,
here, where two legs pressed
against two legs become six legs—
and that is not an impossible math.
I could believe the world only wants
to double. The hay field rising
into seed. The June bugs' dumb love
lifting the night to its feet.

BECOMING
THE
BOY

First, let me admit I am a counterfeit.
A sleek composite. The fourth
meal of the day is paraphernalia.
Which is another way to say, I learned
how to *man,* and I worry
when I'm not careful, I drown out
the seven parts of me
with one abominable baritone. *Should*
sounds so much like *shove,*
doesn't it? It gutters the cold rain
and dumps it on your head.
The soil grows whatever it's fed.
Everything entering the ear takes root.
And speaking of dirt, think
of the dandelion weed—those
little puffs blundering the backyard
with their furry spray lifting to flight.
All it takes is a weak fiasco of wind.
But first, the bulb must bloom yellow—

and pretty even—from a knot
as tight as solitude. And still it scatters
like a fist of warm dice. You too
began curled and cooed awake,
then some blue lung began to chant
a boy should this and *a boy should that,*
and you shouldn't listen, little
corn-shuck, it's a strange song,
mostly sad and hard to dance to.

STRAWBERRIES

FOR

DINNER

Good for the strawberry
for wearing all its seeds on its skin—
too few things say *here's all of me*
like that—not the apple
and its wooden center stones,
not the peach's chipped-tooth pit,
not me in my muddy work shirts,
which I generally ditch
after slumping home at the end of the day
the instant I hear the front door click.
So tired I become working days like this,
I could believe the mime's
gloved hands pressed against
the almost plastic case
placed one foot around him.
Limit is a cocky fellow:
a pallbearer in a vibrant suit.
He named his daughter Bootstrap.
He loves the word "retirement."

He thinks the myth of Icarus
should be printed on the back
of every birth certificate.
That's a cautionary tale I think
he's wrong about. The boy fell. He did.
But what about the blooming hurt
gnawing at his shoulders as he rose?
It must have been excruciating.
His comfort melted long before the wings.
There must have been a moment
he could go no further,
and yet, he did.

ODE

TO

THE

GROTESQUE

Predawn cold, and the jet stream of breath
jumps from the snout. The skin's final form
could be blistered. So say the hands. So says
the bark that half-moons the split log.
So says the ax head and sweat-lacquered shaft.
A whole cauldron of steam can rise
from the humped shoulders when the body
becomes the blade. One can look villainous,
but what if beauty is the beginning of a terror
we can barely stand? So says Rilke. So say
the Cyclops, the ogre, and the monster
taunted by flame. There was a time
I was afraid of him—this father
carrying wood in his arms like a babe.

MEMORIAL

The trick to standing
alone through the night

is to whittle a lump
of wood thinking *boat*.

Another trick
is to burn whatever

refuses the shape
of a hull

and to stare
into the flame

until the frail wood
becomes it.

The trick is to stand
completely still

as a protest
against the waves

stealing the shore,
or another father,

or the harbor factories,
where the machines

hum to imitate
the shells imitating

the sound of the sea.
If you press a thumb

against a flashlight
you'll illuminate the blood

like a stained
glass window.

If you stay still
the tide will fasten

to the back
of your knees.

The trick to standing
alone through the night

is to become a monument
to the shore,

and the fathers,
and the harbor factories,

where the machines
hum to imitate

the shells imitating
the sound of the sea.

Try this: take two fingers
and find the point

where two ribs join
like a flying buttress.

Stay, and the sand
will lock around

your waist; the riptide
will fold you down;

a steeple will peek
like a bud

from your back.

OSIRIS

ODE

If all I ever become
is twenty-eight
stalks of corn,
that would be enough,
I think. And if
a raccoon comes
to shuck a few of me
in the night, or even
at noon, then, listen,
that is good. But maybe
the diligent groundskeeper
of the cemetery
hates me, the corn of me,
and would rather
drive the mower
with its wide steel well
and carousel of shearing
right over me. Corn
the irritant, corn

like a small patch
of stubble the razor
brushes over on the lumpy
Adam's apple. What's orderly
is intoxicating, I get that.
I button up my shirt
after a shower and feel
as though I've got it together.
But maybe it doesn't rain
the year of my death.
My friends plant the seeds
ceremoniously in curved rows,
but even the grass
turns brown. With nothing
to cut, the groundskeeper
cleans the office and scrapes
the moss off the oldest stones
with a dull toothbrush.
Then at least he'll be forced

to sit in the shade eventually.
Even hell must have its respite.
With enough time even he
will have to learn
how to whistle.

THE
THIRD
COMMANDMENT

Some think the cuss
a prelude to a smoky
eternity, and maybe I'm
a little smug, a little
ruffled, to not believe
I'll be strapped naked
to the rack and prodded
with little tridents
just for whispering *goddamn,*
but there are moments
that empty the well-stocked
pantry of my hyperbole,
and there are moments that drop
an invisible bell around
my head and let it ring—and goddamn—
the boy was pushed into this world
and delivered to her chest, wet
and serrating my every theory
of the possible, and bewilderment

came shaped like a pink mouth
to which was slipped
a pink nipple, and goddammit,
the country of amazement
has no lexicon or address—
that country's charter
was written in a single breath.

ODE

TO

THE

ODES

Hey Steve, do you ever think
to write a letter
to the board of selectmen
elected to the blue city
our language makes?
I'd write "Shame on you
who say I should think
like a mourner in a funeral procession—
one sad thought
in front of the other;
I'd rather bumble down
the avenues like I've got
a beefy bourbon
bastard-slapping my veins!"
Because, Steve, you ever
had that almost clavicle snap
bubble of thought
that the round
of your partner's nostril

is just as perfect
as the wheels
on the carts
in the cobble streets
of Babel? I don't know
if I'm making much sense here,
but this morning
my honey hunny
kissed me on the lips
all skunk breath and beautiful.
And Steve, does it ever come to you
like a vanilla-scented wind—
this happiness? Does it
tug at your throat
until out pops a pigeon,
scum-soaked and carrying
a love note
you didn't know
you could write?

CONCEIVING

THE

CHILD

I wanted to say a word of praise
and for that word to grow suddenly
physical. There was a tingling
in the cellar and I wanted to sketch
the image concealed in the dark.
I know little of the crude mechanics
that double us, but I wanted
the blunt eloquence gripping my finger.
The everyday lyric. Impossible
as winding a clock with my throat's
green fiddle, strange as planting
a whole grassy range if I sneezed,
I am spellbound—spellbound—
by what the body will dream.

THE

COULD

BE

Even through closed windows the world
smells like woodstove this morning.
It could be a neighbor's burn pile.
It could be a windstorm and a power line
fallen to a fresh pile of leaves.
I don't know. I do know
there's a frowning boy
who lives in my breast pocket.
He sometimes climbs up my collarbone
to make his little sad hush
about danger and decency.
He's always trying to prune
the chimney vine of me.
The cookies-on-the-top-shelf
-and-the-child's-taut-fingertips of me.
It's hard work, and sometimes
when he's through he lies down
in the rough bassinet of my hands
and sleeps. Just listen: even our enemies

whimper a little in dreams.
Quiet now, little aardvark who roots
the nonsense away. Sleep, little gardener
of my soon enough grave.

FICTION

If I get the story right,
my mother's grief

will melt back into sand—
just enough for a shoreline

the size of her driveway.
We could hold our shoes

by their heels without talking.
In this version, I know

the password to leaven
the latch of fingers

wrapped around aluminum.
I hold a compact mirror

up to her nose to see the fog
of the living. If I get the story

right, a fog will settle
over the shore and there

will be no other place to look
but at each other.

THE
MAIN
EVENT

In this corner the god of Muzak,
and this corner the god of moon-wild
crooning. The ideology of shaved lawns
wears the blue trunks, and the hay field
wears the red. The stroke vs. my father
lasted only one round. It smuggled
a switchblade into the ring, but his fist
was quicker. The welterweights
are the hardest to predict—to-do list
vs. Saturday morning, sidewalk vs. the knees—
but the crowd doesn't come out for those.
Just listen to how they cheer for the champ,
Old Mercy, as he walks to the ring,
no robe glittering his name.

MONARCH
ON
MILKWEED

The milkweed doesn't
pull milk from the dirt,
but it looks like it might,
and my friend Andy
tells me Monarchs
flit from Mexico
and breed five generations
before they reach here,
in Indiana, where
I'm vain enough
to think I, too,
must have died five
or so times
before arriving
at this simple cloud
prettying the roadside ditch,
and too often I become
the staccato roll
of a snare drum,

my trill and shuffle
toward absence,
where the milkweed
is not—or rather
the milkweed is,
and I am not—
where the rain
feeds a seed
into an ivory plume,
and Monarchs roost
in the backyard
where I emptied
the reeking
kitchen scraps
so they might
once again bloom.

ODE
TO
TWO
SYLLABLES

I say hooray to whatever inspired Ashley
to say *Ashley* was her favorite word
in the whole damn language—
the gumption to dredge up
a little self-praise there,
to toss aside the complicated lexis
chiseled into a fat book of English
over all these hundreds of years. Because
what would it be like to taste your own name
like sugared green tea forty-seven times a day?
To sit by a brook and probably hear
Ashley squeezed out of each
foamy bubble? *Ashley* in the willow wind
and car horn just the same. Poor Geraldine
and Bartholomew. Poor words
like "pulchritudinous," which, I'm told,
means "beauty" but hides that meaning
like a single blue bean in the goulash
of a soggy burrito. I say hooray for anything

as simple as two syllables. To the ease
of the early light kittened
through kitchen curtains,
and the Zamboni slow
in the buckwheat grow.
I say hooray to Ashley,
and to the vigor of joy
sequestered in my palms
that tingles like a star
when I clap them together.

ODE

TO

DREAMING

THE

DEAD

Come to the stage and be
your cartoonish self,
says the dream,
says the tiny impressionist
in the cerebellum,
says the frontal lobe,
or whatever gray nook
sets out a few
chaise lounges
for the gone.
There is a feeling
like snapping a sheet
out over a bed.
There is the silence
of a sheet settling.
And if you haven't
felt it, you will—
says the aneurism,
say the rebel cells,

says the lightning strike
and its proud father,
the thunder, which bellows,
good boy, now again.
When I dream
of my dead, I wake
in a sweat and sit
in the kitchen
and listen to the low
radio while the milk
warms. And sitting there,
I have wished it were law
that each person
before they die
record one song—just one—
and if they couldn't sing
they could blow
a terrible trumpet
or kazoo—it wouldn't

matter since such
clamor could be hummed
along to—a little
last whistle and testament,
maybe, a little ditty
infusing the dark rooms
which are too quiet
without them.
And if you're waiting
for the moment
this poem pivots
into joy, I'm sorry,
it's not coming this time,
I thought it might
here in this quiet kitchen,
but it didn't
and that's all right.
All I want is to hear
them hum a tune—

my dead which populate
the dream like a mute
chorus of horses,
for which I unlatch
the barn gate,
and point to the open
field, and click
my tongue, but which
only stand there
staring at the grass.

OPENING
LECTURE
AT
THE
CONSTELLATION
INSTITUTE

When you draw shapes in the night sky,
it will help if you remember
that your pencil passes through matter
we can't see, or name, but know exists.
It will help if you imagine the bright spots
as your parents, your past lovers,
or enemies. Perhaps you will draw
a bull out of your string of breakups,
then use three stars to draw a spear.
By your senior year, you should be able
to outline at least one flower
while studying the history
of dictators. No dippers.
We have enough of those.
The sky is full of empty reservoirs.
We've noticed the sad have a strange desire
to draw things patriotic—the flag
with its flat bars draping the hemisphere,
or a bald eagle with its wide wings

grazing both horizons. It will help
if you resist this craving to claim
the whole sky. It's rude, frankly,
and you will be unpopular.
Most importantly, you'll miss
what happens when the many
separate shapes intertwine.

ELEGY

In the water left from the waitress's rag,
I made James's face:

pinched salt for the scar
below the eyebrow,

a fleck of pepper for a freckle,

bent straw for the bridge of the nose.

The trouble with my over-easy eggs
was their thin skins broke

with a touch of a butter knife.

The trouble with my coffee
was it took the cream and changed.

The trouble with me is I can arrange
three words however I please:

this isn't it

It isn't this

Isn't it this

Isn't this it

JUST
LIKE
THAT

I am employed by loss
as a doll maker
who pleads with his dolls
to breathe. The staccato tap
of the snare drum,
the fingersnap,
the leaves cracked
beneath the boots,
all sound like facts
to support a thesis
on the sudden
signature of grief.
I've lain on this couch
a long time and don't want
to get up. Today, it's enough
to be a couch. To watch
the ceiling beams
do absolutely nothing.
I love how they tell the lie

of the sturdy. How
they make me believe
this house won't suddenly collapse.
Like when a magician
shuffles your card
back to the deck
and pulls it out again.
It's as if he says, *You thought
this world was chaos, huh?
Well here's a trusty talisman.*
But that's just a trick,
I guess, and nothing
says the magician's thumb
won't slip and lose its place
and pull the one-eyed jack
instead of your two.
But at least this time
he got it right. At least
the fruit trees fruited.

At least the flowers curtseyed.
At least this gourd of glow
is spinning. At least
this day is like
the one before,
by which I mean
it happened.

AFTER
FORECLOSURE

I am the stowaway
the captain tied

to the deck
and tattooed blue,

head to toe,
just to remind the others

of half
the shadow

of half the whale.
Soon enough,

we all learn
the fist is the uncle

of the heart,
and I am changing

my name to *Blue Isle,*
to *Blue Savior.*

I believe words
have a mouth

with sharp teeth,
and I am learning

how gently
to lift them.

What if we all
traced checkerboards

into the silt
with the heels

of our shoes?
The whole shore

a tapestry
of boxes.

What if we
said *King me*?

THE
NAME
OF
MY
BANKER

My banker's name
is lodged in my diaphragm
and this makes it hard to breathe.
It's tied as a red string
around my pointer finger.
Sometimes my banker asks
me to call her *Jill*. Sometimes
Jackie. We are happy.
She has something
she wants to give me.
My banker calls me
by my pet name: *Sir.*
When distance is necessary,
she wants me to call her *Banker,*
simply, and we sit at a coffee shop
or somewhere public
so I won't make a scene.
There is a name I call my banker
that sounds like a music box

missing a lid. The name of my banker
is *Boot*. The name of my banker
is *Bill*. The name of my banker
is *Baker* and he wants to give me
an extra roll he pressed
with his own two hands.
Sometimes he calls me randomly
and the name of my banker
sounds like straw
shoved in the chest
of a scarecrow,
because even my banker
speaks as if there
is the name of a banker
lodged in his diaphragm.
This must make it hard for him
to breathe. For all I know,
my banker might say *please,*
again and again in the shower

and with the car windows
rolled up. Or, like me,
he might have scraped his elbow
as a boy and it didn't bleed.
Not exactly. It looked like it might.
And he may have spent
the whole afternoon
wondering why,
when the skin opened,
everything wouldn't
come rushing out.

THE
LORDS
AND SERFS
OF SAND
AND SEA

As kids, we conjured jungle gyms into whaling ships,
    and depending on the jobs of our parents,

one of us played captain, and one of us played anchor,
    and sometimes we stood on our toes in the crow's nest,

gazing at a glint of the sun on the sea
    through shoreline mansion windows.

This is a country with whole stretches of beach
    sealed in a purse with a gold lock and bone key.

Salt cardiogrammed the levee, and I could sit
    on a dock until someone told me not to.

In the dream my sister remembers best,
    she's standing beside a wooden fence

that stretches and curves the whole coastline.
     She wants to get through, and she's found a hole

the size of a thumbtack. She scatters her clothes,
     and raises her hands. She peels each layer of skin,

unspooling the fretwork of veins and bone slowly,
     until she is one floating mass hovering the beach.

My sister then slips through the hole in the fence as whatever
     liquid she is—as whatever benediction—and the ocean

dismantles the helix that makes her.

SOVEREIGNTY

The burn pile threw our bodies in dark shapes against the grass.

A tendril braid of smoke swirling. We were learning

we could stand stock-still with a hose but couldn't

keep our silhouettes from dancing.

In the fields, littered hay bales still caught the wind,

if even just slightly. The splintered skiff hull,

belly-up on bank blocks, still went slick each storm.

And if the wind grew thick in the night with barn swallows,

they populated our sleep as we breathed what couldn't

belong to us: *field furrow, coop roof, stonewall strewn,*

and *moss pocked.* I was learning I was a flicker

in the mirror of a corn husk. I was learning

to walk barefoot, touching every ghosted hay mound

with my soft and makeshift hands.

DEAD
MAN
FLOAT

was a game, was the back-
humped and limb-stiff hover
until something inside the body
said *enough*. Then it was time
to watch. To count aloud
what might be the last
seconds of living. His body,
underwater, blurred.
In the distance, the ocean
flattened like a lifeline.
There was an unspoken rule
not to help. To need help
was a weakness. We
were boys. It was a game
we made ourselves.

GROCERY
STORE
MANAGER

Manager likes to find ways
to entertain himself.
He'll work the register too.
Just like us. He won't
step in the freezer,
but will greet patrons
at the door. Manager
asks me to start wearing pants
without holes in our
quarterly meeting. The meeting
is held on the break room couch
with many upholstery holes.
I can look purposeful
like a weathervane.
Then he says, *I know you don't*
want to be here, and Manager admits
he wanted to be an architect,
and even went to school for it,
but says this to the floor,

quietly, and so, like the floor,
I do not speak. The floor nods.
Manager went to the produce guy's
metal concert once—he didn't
seem to care for it, but he went.
I can respect that. *Sometimes
I wish I could just stock cereal*
is not something Manager says,
because he doesn't have to.
Manager doesn't have to ask
if I too feel like a coatrack
nailed to the floor.

ODE

TO

ALTERNATIVES

Hey Kevin, I know
I'm always talking,
but look at those
two little boys who
don't know any better—
they're using a king
as a pawn, a pawn
as a knight, a queen
as a bishop—and isn't
not knowing the rules
just beautiful?
Because really,
where's the joy
in shouldering night
into workday
when we can be the carpenters
of unmade things,
flailing our hammers
whichever way we please

in the dark? I'm sorry
I'm talking too much
for this chess game,
but I get nervous.
Are there people out there
who say we're dangerous?
When the sun echoes
off the thousands
of windshields
locked in the morning commute,
do you sometimes feel
like we're dressed for a party
we couldn't ever hope
to be invited to?
Do the idling engines
deafen you?
Kevin, are you sure you want
to trade your knight
for a rook? Why is it

that once we take
our hand off of it,
we can't take it back?

HONEYSUCKLE

The part of me
that thinks honeysuckle
must be pleased
with such a name
is an ignorant ass.
Honeysuckle doesn't care,
and, really, it would leaven
every stone just to get to the light.
It would spread
like a perfumed disease
over the garden,
shadowing the lettuce,
because it would be
compelled to. What a failure
it would make without a thought—
just how the thoughtless
and innocent sickness
streams through my friend Leah
and makes her tired

this morning, and almost
all the time. I could hear
how spent even leaving a message
on my phone made her.
I want to find a wooden ladle
and take the afternoon
to pinch into it
every amber bead of sweet
from a honeysuckle.
I want to cradle my haul
with one hand
gripping the handle,
and the other hand
cupping the spoon,
and I want to lift my foot
to knock gently
on her door.

A
LEXICON
TO FILL
A
RAIN
GAUGE

Shifting wheat. Cattail seed
sprung like birdshot.

The tarp horsewhip
above the half-worked

harvest in sheaves.
Here again, the air

turned nickel, season
of dropcloth sky.

What's another word
for *idle* that's not *sloth*?

For *regret* that's not *failure*?
The horse bucked

her birthing colt
snap neck

against the concrete.
What's another word

for *salvage* that's not *storm*?
The wind turned sinew white.

The cornstalks bristled.
What's another word

for *jubilee* that's not
written in mud

and a thousand concussions
on the coop's tin roof?

THE
GAME
AS
GOOD
MEDICINE

I say hooray to the no-look dish
and the ball kissing
the glass before netting.
And I say hooray, too,
to the backpedal then—
that brief chapter of joy
the squeak of the sneakers
read aloud from the court.
Today, I want to love
the loop of the game,
the ball, and whatever
sends me volleying back
and forth so blissfully.
Isn't it good to do
one thing well
then try to do it again?
Think the looped beat
and the hip bone
like a round pestle

grinding the pelvis
into a lover's. Think
the lavender perennial,
pulsing its purple
each spring, to which
you might lower your face.
I first ran the loop
with abandon on the recess court,
then sweated through
half of history class
where all the books
read in a straight line
from left to right.
I remember chapter one
led to chapter two
and we reached our present
in June. But the problem
is that math says straight lines
stretch forever. And the problem

with distance is it makes one forget.
The problem is honesty
comes shaped like a circle.
Like a loop. Like a low hum
of reverb shaking wild these days.

A

BRIEF

HISTORY

OF

EVOLUTION

When did my brother first let his toes
hang over the lip of a quarry cliff,

unbutton his shirt, and show Evel
Knievel's letter of recommendation

written on his bare muscled chest?
When did he learn that a rainbow

would appear on a wall
from light shot off a carving knife?

Tonight, the boy he's put inside a hospital
might tell you my brother

is the sound of knuckle slapped
against an eye socket,

the small smell of propane
leaking from a tank

attached to a house. I remember
he would race a finger-long mouse

against a tail of flame
and I would watch. Before

the mouse could reach the cheese
or the flame could reach

the can of lighter fluid,
he would hopscotch on the fuse,

saying it was important that neither won,
important to lift the mouse

back to the bag so he
could use the thing again.

IN
THIS
PHOTO,
JAMES

is sitting on a green couch
with his hand raised
like a conductor's
quieting the orchestra—
palm flat and held out.

It looks a little
like he could be
closing a window.

He's laughing,
or is smiling anyways,
with his head dipped
a little to the left.

I remember how we once
climbed over a pasture's
barbed-wire fence

because we wanted
to be someplace
we didn't belong.

James's shin caught a barb,
but the cut was thin,
and he said it didn't matter.

Let's just go back, I said.

And he held up his hand and said,
No, *really, it's fine.*

ODE
TO
THE
UNSAYABLE

There was a word
I was taught
not to say
in the gym, or on
the basketball court,
the playground,
and sometimes
at home, and so
I took to picturing
this word
locked in my gut
as a sunbeam-starved
and skinny
dungeon inmate.
When I did
lift a torch
to the wrought-iron door
where this
yardbird jangled

his chains
like hell-smithed
windchimes, he held
his palms open
to a bath of light
washing the dank stones.
And yes, maybe
there are words
we should smother
to oblivion,
but what
if I told you
the word I kept
locked wasn't
some expletive
to ruffle
the tighty-whities
of the principal,
but was, in fact,

love? Love, the unsayble.
Love, the destitute
and hungry. If you
were a boy
in America
maybe they beat
this word
into the dungeon
of you, too.
The gym,
the playground,
and sometimes
at home.
Maybe they cracked
their fist
against your temple.
You learned to focus
on tufts of grass
that seemed

to litter the dirt.
Who was it
who told me
the tongue
has no bones,
so we've got
to learn
how to hold it?
My tongue can do
amazing things
when my love
wants it. I'll say it
again: *love*.
And again: *love*.

A

BRIEF

HISTORY

OF

PATIENCE

A hundred or so lobster pots cut loose

and chock-full of dead catch. Broken jaw

of a pier. Summers I learned

what once was buried just as easily

might surface: car keys, caulking gun,

whale rib the size of a park bench.

Boys rode their boats like bulls. Were bucked

and washed ashore with half the throttle fast beneath

the foam-white knuckles of their fists.

Salt hitched my hair and scraped my skin.

Bottles in the cooler clinked like dice.

Nights, I would wait for the first fish

to swallow the hook. The trick, I learned,

was not to force it, was to let the fish feel the pain

that comes from blindness and mistake.

IN
THE
HEADWINDS
OF
A
FABLE

My friends and I live with small patches of hurt,
       and I sit on my couch in the early morning
and write a word, then another, and imagine
       if this sentence stretches long enough, it might break
into a road with little rumble strips and ditch grass
       and guardrails for all of us to hop in my car
to drive along, our pockets of worry torn from our shirts
       and flung to the faded dotted lines that disappear
a little more every day, because they must, like this road
       must turn to gravel, like this gravel must turn to dirt,
until it narrows into a hairline trail, and we park
       and bury the keys, and follow one another
down the thinning walk, one foot in front of the other
       until we stop, for no other reason but to stop
like pack mules twittering shoulders in the May moon cold,
       and Julie casually picks at a cigarette burn on her wrist,
and Sam watches the stars charismatically collapse,
       and he isn't thinking of the neon shine

from his brother's moped skittering away on the city street,
  and nobody's looking down at their feet,
we're watching Julie who lifts the scab like a secret
    to block out the moon, all of the moon, and we're
watching still as she takes away the pinch in her fingers,
    as the scab stays there suspended in the air,
perfectly fastened to the light, and we all take turns
    looking through this paper-thin wafer
like an unsightly telescope, this stained glass window
    of skin so vital and durable and true.

LONG
GONE
ONES

Do these windows
fog with you,
always watching
as I fumble
over the apartment's
exposed nails?
I can cut your names
with the thaw
of a finger.
I can see
the whole town
through those letters.

A
BRIEF
HISTORY
OF
SILENCE

In the dark, I could read the stiff salt
of your cheeks like Braille. What more
could anyone want than to crease history
into a paper boat and feed the thing

to a riptide? I wore a tooth-pocked tongue
filled with old curses. You too.
Thought as many wishes
as there are pills in a pharmacy.

When I slept, my dreams
shook like a brood from a mob,
the sheets spindled into a tapestry,
the fridge lumbered to life down the hall.

NEAR

THE

END

He stands in a bubble in the backyard.

The bubble is large, and so only looks
like an oily wall.

This whole life
behind this one thin wall,

and he presses his hand through.

The wall feels like a small waterfall on his wrist.

It is a Wednesday. Now his arm is on
the other side. Now his chest and his head.

The air smells of pine. The back door
is painted yellow.

And he stands there
trying to understand
why he hasn't noticed that before.

LORD,

I play a game some nights:
quarter an apple
and toss each piece
to a corner of the yard,
turn off the lights,
and wait for what might arrive.

ODE

TO

THE

ETHER

How many invisibles
ferret through this ruckus
of me? What phantom things
fill every empty corner
of my salt-bloated simmer?
Lately, the weekdays each drop
a heavy rock in my satchel,
and I'm a sad type
of wind-up mailman
with a key sewn into
the center of my back.
But this morning,
at the table and over
a bowl of steel-cut oats,
every last fist of air
my lips wrought
into a litany of sad
was taken into your lungs too,
and turned around light and clean.

The same air that carried
my complaint, carried
your salve, which I take
to mean that the air was not
just mine alone, and that,
I think, is a beautiful thing.

THE
CLAM

That shell like a frozen ripple;
that living stone burrowed in the silt;
I was wary of it—how it must
live static, an anchor, and what
is life without a little recklessness,
without a little touch of mess
to pivot up the day—the lightning
plucked like a wrong note
brightens the sky—I believed
the metronome had already died,
and circles were the saddest shapes,
and who would lasso their finger
with a little silver ring? Only fools
or lunatics—and tonight
restlessness rips me from sleep.
I watch the baby breathe. I imitate
stillness, for fear the antique floor

might creak. The clam opens up
to let the current in,
and by doing so, lives.

UDDER

Who wasn't amazed
by the tassel-like teats of cows
as a wee one? What's
stranger than a cotton candy,
slipper-soft mound
sagging between two bony legs?
Never mind squeezing it
made milk. Never mind
the calf ramming it
with its sledgehammer snout.
Is there anything as naked?
To this day, it makes
me want to shuck my shirt.
To be tugged. To be a balloon
that won't burst. The skin
elastic. And I love the way
the cows gather under the field's
only tree and its raft of shade.
Maybe a twitch of a tail

to swat the green flies away,

but otherwise, they're still,

the way I've been only

a handful of times, I think,

which is not enough,

though, this morning, in the garden

pinching off the basil,

and propping up the tomatoes,

and lifting off two caterpillars

with my ungloved fingers

to let them walk off

onto the grass, I was at least

silent, and listened a little

to the wind trilling the thousand

leaves of the peach tree,

and I breathed. This breath.

This blood. These wet gears

sliding exactly as they're supposed to.

What's stranger than the soft

mounds in the chest?
The lungs' dawdling rollick
tugs the air. This
drizzling delicate cadence.
The body fills with it
like milk. Never mind
the last exhale. Think
about the first. And the second.
They gather like pearls
on a string. This quiet,
handless work.

NOTES

The line "what if beauty is the beginning of a terror/we can barely stand?" in "Ode to the Grotesque" refers to Rainer Maria Rilke's "First Elegy" from *Duino Elegies* (trans. Gary Miranda).

"Ode to the Odes" is for Steve Scafidi.

"Opening Lecture at the Constellation Institute" is for Michelle Peñaloza.

"Grocery Store Manager" is for Joshua Gottlieb-Miller and Nigel O'Shea.

"Ode to Alternatives" is for Kevin Eldridge.

"Honeysuckle" is for Leah Nielsen.

"Udder" is for Ross Gay.

ACKNOWLEDGMENTS

Thank you to the editors of the following publications, where poems in this manuscript have appeared, sometimes in earlier forms:

The Adriot Journal: "Becoming the Boy," "Dead Man Float." *Best New Poets 2009:* "A Brief History of Patience." *Cellpoems:* "Lord." *Colorado Review:* "Honeysuckle." *Copper Nickel:* "Conceiving the Child." *Cream City Review:* "Ode to Dreaming the Dead." *Gulf Coast:* "Near the End," "Elegy." *Hayden's Ferry Review:* "A Brief History of Evolution." *The Journal:* "A Brief History of Silence." *Memorious:* "The Lords and Serfs of Sand and Sea," "A Lexicon to Fill a Rain Gauge." *Meridian:* "Long Gone Ones." *Mid-American Review:* "Memorial." *Minnesota Review:* "Fiction." *The Paris-American:* "Ode to the Grotesque." *Pinwheel:* "After Foreclosure." *Poetry Northwest:* "Grocery Store Manager." *Redivider:* "The Name of My Banker." *The Rumpus:* "Keel," "Ode to the Odes." *Southern Indiana Review:* "Ode to Two Syllables," "In the Headwinds of a Fable." *Toad:* "Ode to Alternatives." *Tupelo Quarterly:* "Osiris Ode," "Ode to the Unsayable." *Vinyl Poetry:* "The Clam," "The Could Be," "The Doubling," "The Game as Good Medicine," "The Third Commandment." *Washington Square Review:* "Sovereignty."

Additionally, some of these poems appeared in the chapbook *Still, the Shore* (YesYes Books, 2013).

Thanks to the many readers and supporters whose insights helped shape this book, including my friends at the Bloomington Community Orchard, the Bread Loaf Writers' Conference, Indiana University, the Sewanee Writers' Conference, and Westfield State University.

Special thanks to Oliver Bendorf, Gabrielle Calvocoressi, Kai Carlson-Wee, Doug Paul Case, Nandi Comer, Kendra DeColo, Kevin Eldridge, Richie Hofmann, Rebecca Gayle Howell, Josh Kalscheur, Steven Kleinman, Kien Lam, Cate Lycurgus, Erika Meitner, Matthew Modica, Ife-Chudeni Oputa, Michelle Peñaloza, Asako Serizawa, Alan Shapiro, Solmaz Sharif, Sarah Suksiri, Katherine Sullivan, Ryan Teitman, Alexander Weinstein, Timothy Welsh, Marcus Wicker, Phillip B. Williams, and Keith Wilson.

Thanks also to my teachers: Romayne Rubinas Dorsey, Michael Filas, Joan Houlihan, Karen Kovacik, Maurice Manning, and Steve Scafidi.

Thanks to Jenna Johnson, her belief in this work, and the great staff at Houghton Mifflin Harcourt.

Thank you for the figs, Ross Gay.

Thank you for the compass, Leah Nielsen.

Thank you for the porch, Kurian Johnson.

Thank you for the love and support, Paul, Linda, Kayla, Gregg, and the whole extended Quincy clan.

Thank you, immeasurably and continuously, to Jennifer and Noah Leonard.